SCIENCE IN OUR WORLD

GROWING *and* CHANGING

Contributory Author
Brian Knapp, BSc, PhD
Art Director
Duncan McCrae, BSc
Special photography
Graham Servante
Special models
Tim Fulford, MA, Head of Design and Technology, Leighton Park School
Editorial consultants
Anna Grayson, Rita Owen
Science advisor
Andrew Burnett, MB.ChB, MRCGP, DRCOG, Family Doctor
Jack Brettle, BSc, PhD, Chief Research Scientist, Pilkington plc
Environmental Education Advisor
Colin Harris, County Advisor, Herts. CC
Production controller
Patricia Browning
Print consultants
Landmark Production Consultants Ltd
Printed and bound in Hong Kong
Produced by *EARTHSCAPE EDITIONS*

First published in the United Kingdom in 1991
by Atlantic Europe Publishing Company Limited
86 Peppard Road, Sonning Common, Reading,
Berkshire, RG4 9RP, UK
Tel: (0734) 723751   Fax: (0734) 724488

Copyright © 1991
Atlantic Europe Publishing Company Limited

Reprinted in 1992

British Library Cataloguing in Publication Data
Knapp, Brian
   Growing and Changing
   1. Growing and Changing – For children
   I. Title   II. Series
   574
          ISBN 1-869860-65-9

All rights reserved. No part of this publication may be reproduced, stored in a retrieval system, or transmitted in any form or by any means otherwise, without prior permission in writing of the publisher, nor be otherwise circulated in any form of binding or cover other than that in which it is published and without a similar condition including this condition being imposed on the subsequent purchaser.

In this book you will find some words that have been shown in **bold** type. There is a full explanation of each of these words on pages 46 and 47.

On many pages you will find experiments that you might like to try for yourself. They have been put in a coloured box like this.

Acknowledgements
The publishers would like to thank the following:
Jonathan Frankel, Irene Knapp, Leighton Park School, Micklands County Primary School, Redlands County Primary School, the Morris family and the Burnett family.

Picture credits
t=top b=bottom l=left r=right

All photographs from the Earthscape Editions photographic library except the following:
Aquila 31t; Jack Jackson 26b; Nigel Phillips 27t, 27b; Tony Pittaway 30, 31b; ZEFA 7t, 7b, 22, 23, 33, 34, 35.

Contents

Introduction	Page	4
In the beginning		6
The early years		8
A sense of proportion		10
High and mighty		12
Racing growth		14
Teeth		16
Bones		18
Familiar feet		20
Filling out		22
Growing older		24
Hatching out		26
From water to land		28
A brand new body		30
Making room for growth		32
Fishy changes		34
Games they play		36
Getting noticed		38
Sprouting into life		40
Leaves		42
Flowering and fruiting		44
New words		46
Index		48

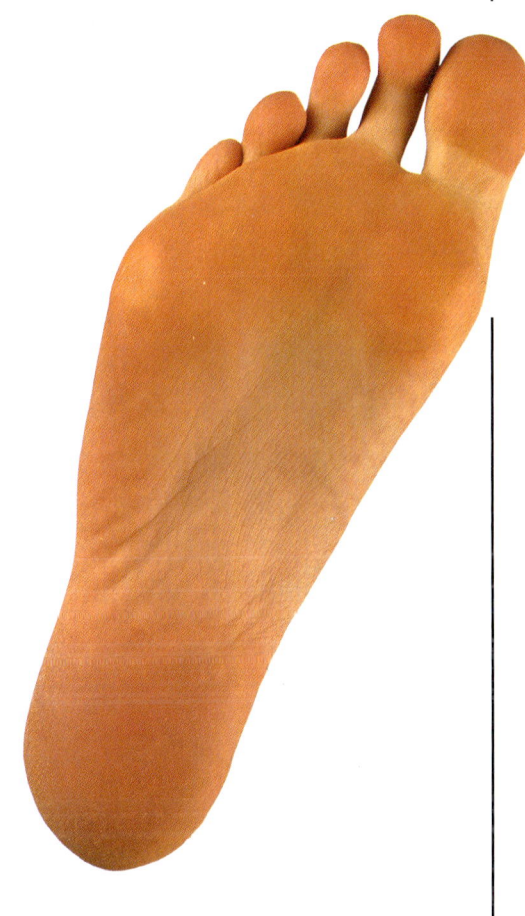
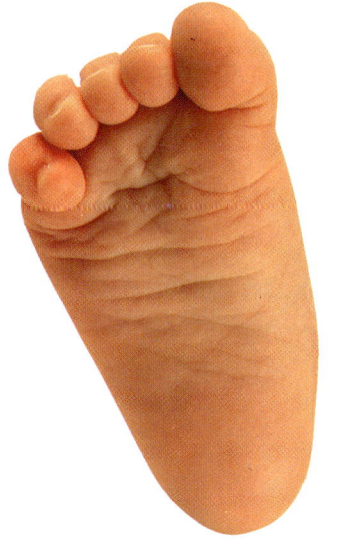

Introduction

fish
page 34

birth
page 6

games
page 36

height
page 12

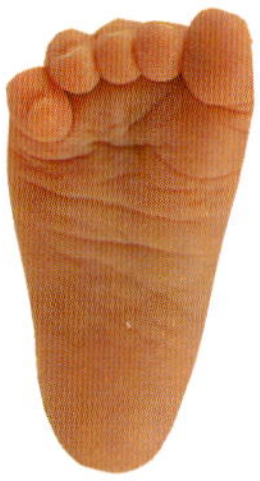

Look at yourself. How much have you changed since your last birthday? Have you grown taller, put on more weight or stayed the same?

The chances are that you have not stayed the same. No living things do. Everything goes through a cycle of life from birth, then youth and maturity to old age. Finally all livings things complete their cycle, die and are replaced by others.

Sometimes change is very clear. A flower can open in a few hours, a shoot can grow tall in a few days, babies begin to crawl around in a few months. But many changes are slower. You may grow a centimetre or two in a year, you may put on a few hundred grammes in the same time.

feet
page 20

sprouting
page 40

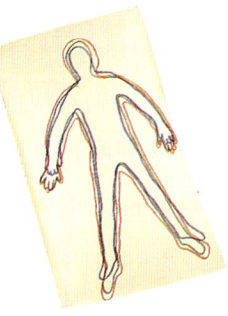

display
page 38

body shapes
page 10

older people
page 24

hatching
page 26

4

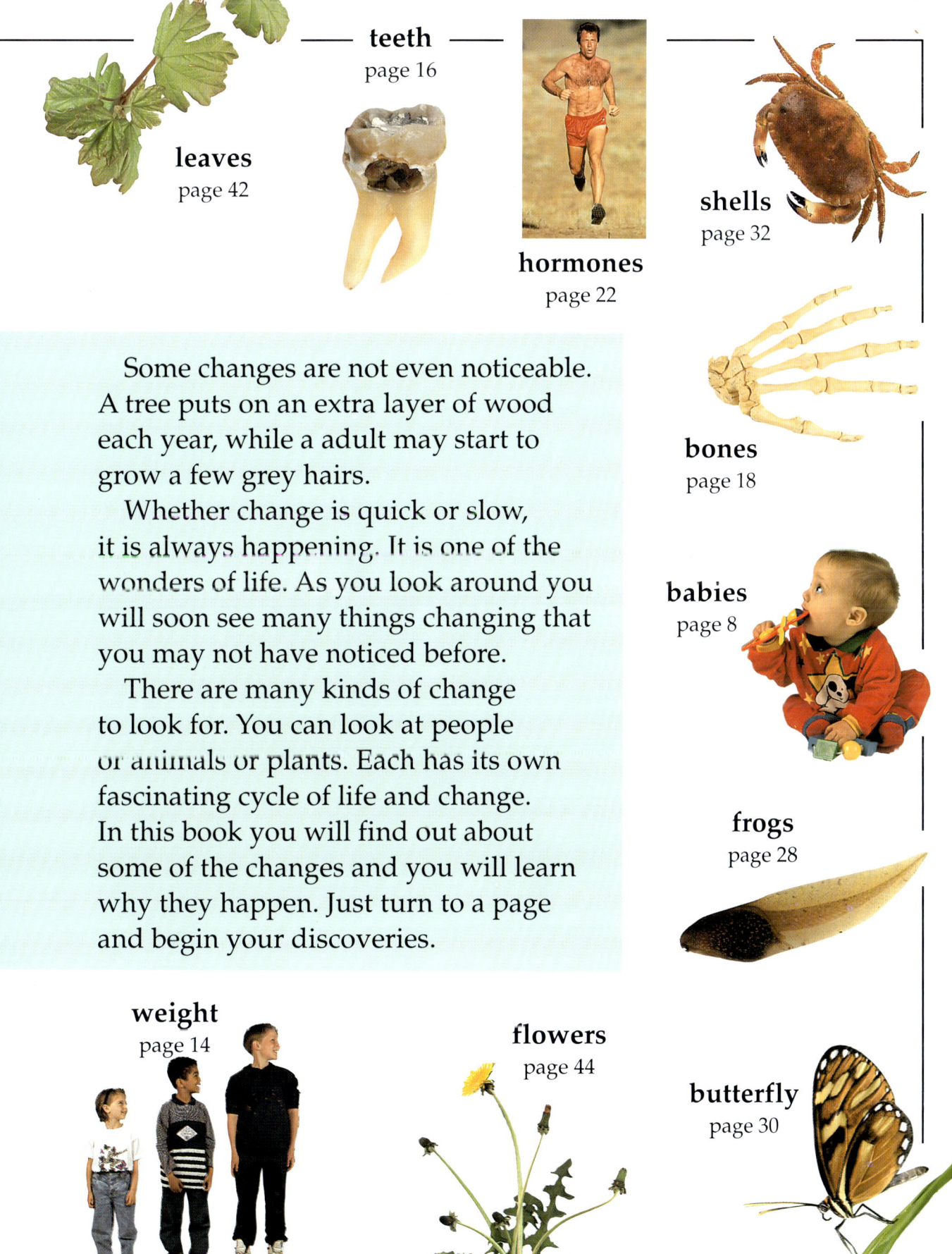

leaves
page 42

teeth
page 16

hormones
page 22

shells
page 32

bones
page 18

babies
page 8

frogs
page 28

Some changes are not even noticeable. A tree puts on an extra layer of wood each year, while a adult may start to grow a few grey hairs.

Whether change is quick or slow, it is always happening. It is one of the wonders of life. As you look around you will soon see many things changing that you may not have noticed before.

There are many kinds of change to look for. You can look at people or animals or plants. Each has its own fascinating cycle of life and change. In this book you will find out about some of the changes and you will learn why they happen. Just turn to a page and begin your discoveries.

weight
page 14

flowers
page 44

butterfly
page 30

5

In the beginning

Each of us begins life as a tiny group of **cells** inside our mothers. The way we grow and change before we are born is the first miracle of life.

A baby grows fastest inside its mother than at any other time. From first cells to birth a baby may increase its weight by three million times!

Compact shape
An unborn baby is curled up into the most compact shape possible.

You can find out about the way an unborn baby is curled inside its mother by curling up like this.

When you are curled up tight you may find it difficult to breathe. Can you think why this does not bother an unborn baby?

As the unborn baby grows inside the **womb**, the mother's shape changes. The picture show the position of an unborn baby

The trials of life
Being pregnant is not an easy matter. As the baby grows inside the womb it is becoming bigger and heavier. This can make life very uncomfortable for the mother. Even ordinary everyday things like putting shoes on can become difficult tasks.

Safe and well

It takes about nine months for a human baby to grow inside its mother. During this time it is kept safe and warm, and is provided with all the necessities of life.

While the baby is in the womb it receives all its food and oxygen from its mother through a tissue called the **placenta**. The baby is attached to the placenta by the **umbilical** cord. The baby's blood flows through the umbilical cord to the placenta.

The remains of your umbilical cord make up your 'belly-button'.

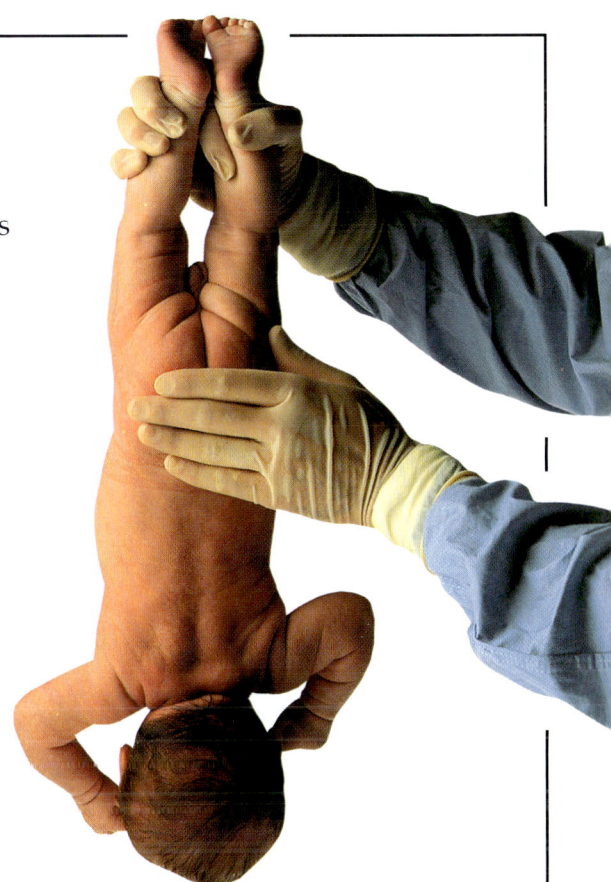

The first breath

Babies are usually born 'upside down' so the head and nose quickly get into the air.

To make sure the baby's airways are clear, it was traditional for doctors to give the newly born baby a gentle smack on the bottom while holding it upside down. Today there are special instruments which clear the air passages more effectively.

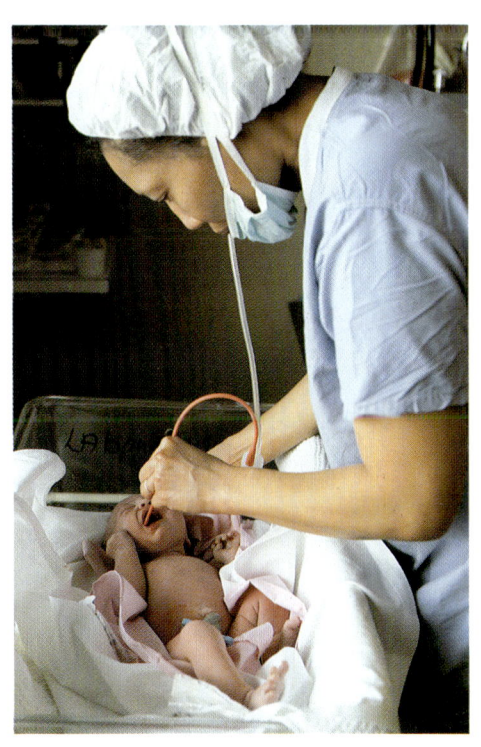

Problems of pregnancy
Find out how difficult and tiring it is to carry an extra weight around your middle. Try tying a three kilogramme bag of potatoes around your middle, then walk around with it for a while.

Does the extra weight make you change the way you hold your back? Do you notice any other problems?

7

The early years

A newborn baby enters the world every few seconds. Wherever they are born, they arrive with all the essential things for a long healthy life. But it will be many years before a baby can look after itself.

During this time many changes will take place and the first stages of learning often depend on the help from other members of the family.

Claire has recognised her mother and you can see she is pleased to see her. She is starting to learn social skills

Arthur is reaching out to touch his father, but he is not yet confident of how far to stretch

Stretching out

A baby has to learn how to use its senses. One of the first senses it develops is its sense of smell. Babies first recognise their mothers by smell.

Soon after, a baby begins to stretch out with its hands and arms, learning how to judge distances.

Baby watch

If you have a baby brother or sister, watch carefully to see the way they play. See what you can find out about the way a baby learns.

Developing senses

Babies put many of their toys in their mouths. This is because the mouth is very sensitive and the sense of touch sends many messages to the brain.

Claire is learning how to co-ordinate her limbs and how to balance. Crawling is the first step in this process

Learning

Many things we do automatically as an older person had to be learned when we were very young.

We use our eyes and hands together to touch things. This is called co-ordination and it is a skill.

Young children have to learn co-ordination. One good way of doing this is by using special games that make learning fun.

A sense of proportion

We are all different. We may vary in the length of our arms and legs, and we are all different heights. Everyone also has a different face. Yet despite all the differences, people of every age have the same basic proportions. Here is how to begin to find out what the proportions are.

Baby face
A baby has all the same features as an older person, but they are in quite different proportions.

If you look at a baby the most striking thing is its eyes. This is because they are much larger compared to the size of its head than an older person.

A baby's head is also large in proportion to its body. Its head will grow, but it starts life well developed because the baby's survival depends on a well developed brain.

Trace changes
Carefully trace off the baby's head from the picture below and then lay the tracing paper over the older girl's head. In this way you will be able to see the changes in proportions more easily.

Age under 1

Age about 11

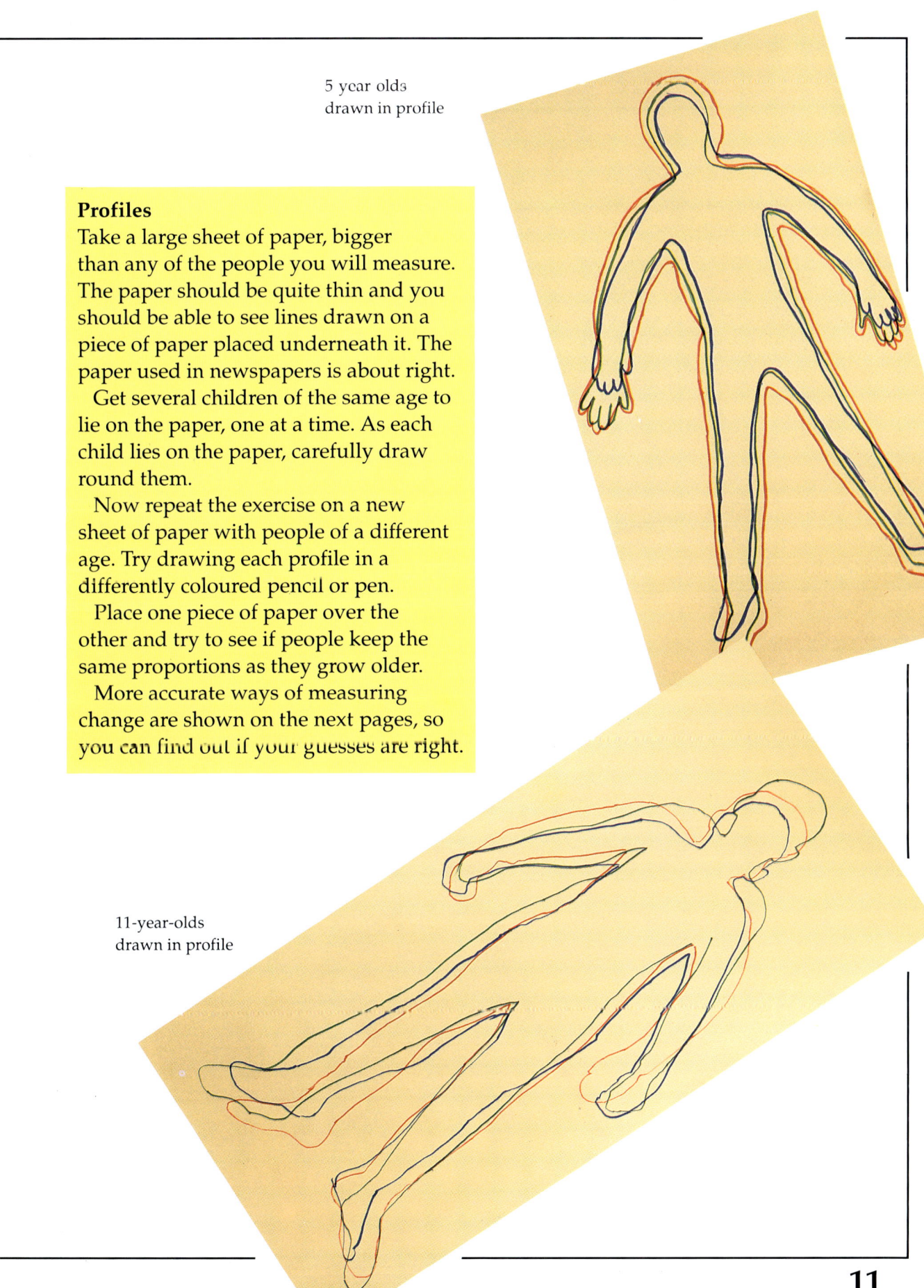

5 year olds drawn in profile

Profiles

Take a large sheet of paper, bigger than any of the people you will measure. The paper should be quite thin and you should be able to see lines drawn on a piece of paper placed underneath it. The paper used in newspapers is about right.

Get several children of the same age to lie on the paper, one at a time. As each child lies on the paper, carefully draw round them.

Now repeat the exercise on a new sheet of paper with people of a different age. Try drawing each profile in a differently coloured pencil or pen.

Place one piece of paper over the other and try to see if people keep the same proportions as they grow older.

More accurate ways of measuring change are shown on the next pages, so you can find out if your guesses are right.

11-year-olds drawn in profile

High and mighty

Measure your school
A school has many people of different ages. You can find out about the **average** height of each year group and perhaps make a chart to show what the changes are like.

In each year group are the girls or the boys taller?

Have you noticed how much taller you are now than last year? Growing upwards happens very quickly and full height is reached by people when they reach their mid teens. They take much longer to fill out and increase their weight.

But growing upwards is not a steady process; it happens in fits and starts. Here's how to chart your height and that of your friends.

This is an accurate scale for measuring heights

In each group of the same aged people there will slight differences in height

A group of people aged about 6

Compare your growth

You can measure your growth every week to see what changes take place. You may find that, if you have been ill, your body doesn't grow as fast. Then, when you are well again you put on a spurt of growth to catch up.

To measure these changes you will need to measure yourself accurately by using the millimetres scale on the ruler. You should also stand in the same way each time, wear no shoes and be perfectly relaxed.

Use the right angle measurer shown here to get the best results. It is easily made from a triangular piece of wood and it can be used against any plain wall.

Place the wood against the wall and mark the position of the base of the triangle.
Next measure the distance from the floor to the mark

A group of people aged about 8

On average, the older group is always taller than the younger ones

A group of people aged about 11

Racing growth

As well as growing upwards, you grow all round as well. You put on weight and you get stronger and bigger muscles, and your hair grows differently.

Profiles give you a general idea of change, but to find out which bits of you grow fastest and why, you need to chart your progress. Here are a few ways of getting accurate measurements.

Strips of wood stuck to the base board

Squared paper

Base board

Accurate measurements
When you measure it is important to be accurate. Here is a simple tool that has been made for measuring the dimensions of feet accurately. You could easily make one for yourself. Can you make other measuring instruments?

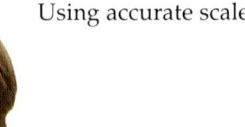
Using accurate scales

Measuring muscle size

Growth chart

Find out the average weight of each age group in your school and compare it with the heights measured on the previous page. Ask a grown-up to help you to make a chart of height and weight using the information given on the right.

Find your weight

What is your weight? Does it change through the day?

Measure yourself on bathroom scales every hour and see what changes you can find. You will have to look carefully at the scale.

Weight varies with what exercise you have been doing, when you eat and when you visit the bathroom.

Ask a grown-up to help you to work out your average weight over a week.

Age 11 years
Height 152 cm
Weight 54 kg

Age 8 years
Height 129 cm
Weight 32 kg

Age 6 years
Height 113 cm
Weight 20 kg

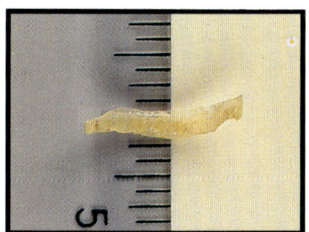

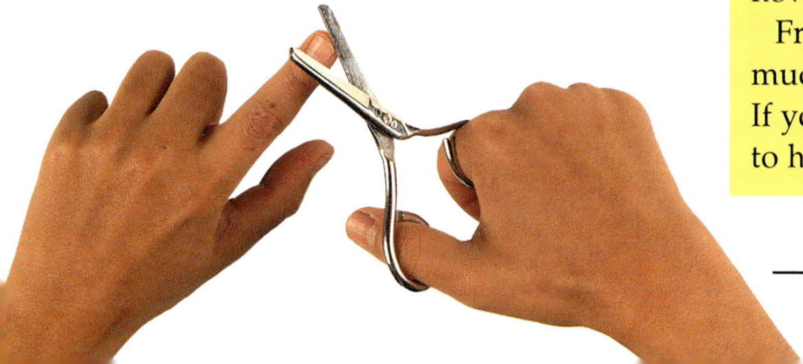

Which grows faster?

Your hair and nails both grow quite quickly, but which grows faster? The hair on your head grows about a centimetre a month. You can use this value to compare hair growth with the growth of your nails.

Cut your nails and make a note of the date. Then, when you cut your nails again, place the clippings on a ruler to find out how much they have grown.

From this you can easily work out how much your nails have grown in a month. If you are not sure how, ask a grown-up to help you.

15

Teeth

The hardest parts of our bodies are teeth and bones. Teeth and bones may seem hard and dead, but they are very much alive. They change size and shape throughout our lives. We even change our teeth completely.

Incisors – chisel-shaped for cutting

The first set
When we are young we have no teeth at all. Babies have no use for teeth. So teeth come through later on, when a baby changes from liquid to solid food.

The period of teething normally occurs when a baby is between 6 and 8 months old. As the teeth break through, or erupt, from the gums they can be painful and cause babies to cry.

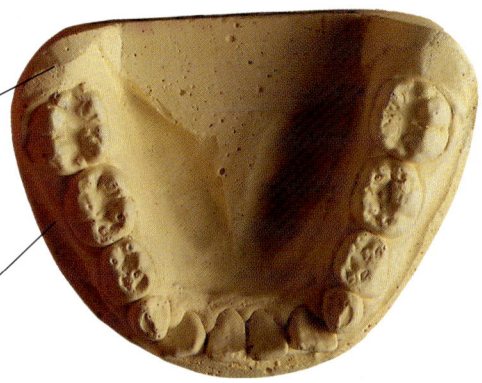

Wisdom teeth appear here

Molars – wide and knobbly for crushing

A young person's teeth

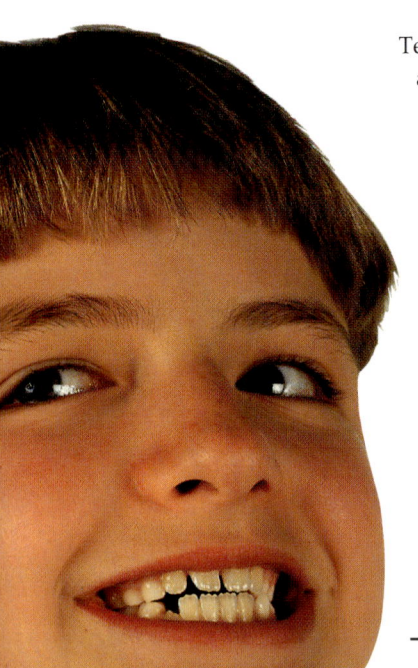

Teeth often erupt at odd angles or in ways that leave gaps. A brace can be fitted by a dentist to help the teeth grow more evenly

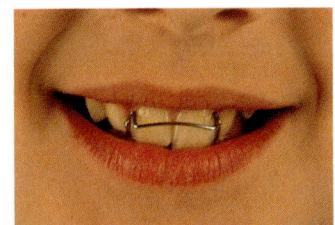

Changing sets
Everyone has two sets of teeth. The first set are called milk teeth, or deciduous teeth. There is only room for 20 teeth at this stage.

The second set of teeth, called permanent teeth, erupt and push out the milk teeth between the ages of 6 to 13.

Later, at age 18-21, the jaw is big enough to accept a final set of four teeth – the wisdom teeth – and these erupt at the back of the mouth.

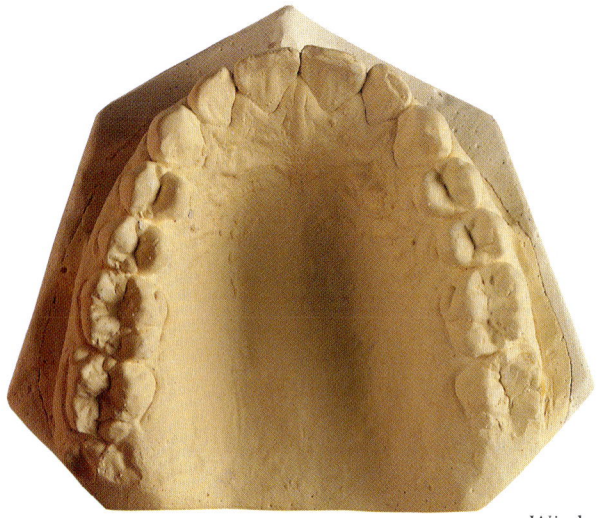

An adult's teeth

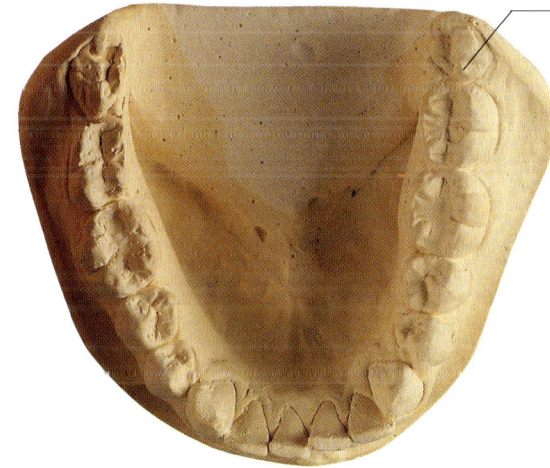

Wisdom teeth

Changing for the worse

Teeth are very complicated structures. The tooth has a hard coating called enamel, but there is a very sensitive material in its centre. This material – called dentine – is connected to the roots by **nerves**.

If you do not look after your teeth, the chances are that the surface enamel will become pitted from attack by acid. Acids are produced as **bacteria** use the sugars left on your teeth after you eat meals, snacks or sweets.

As the enamel becomes damaged the dentine is quickly attacked. This is the stage when the nerves feel the decay and toothache sets in. The only remedies are fillings or extraction.

Cleaning teeth regularly prevents most of these unpleasant changes.

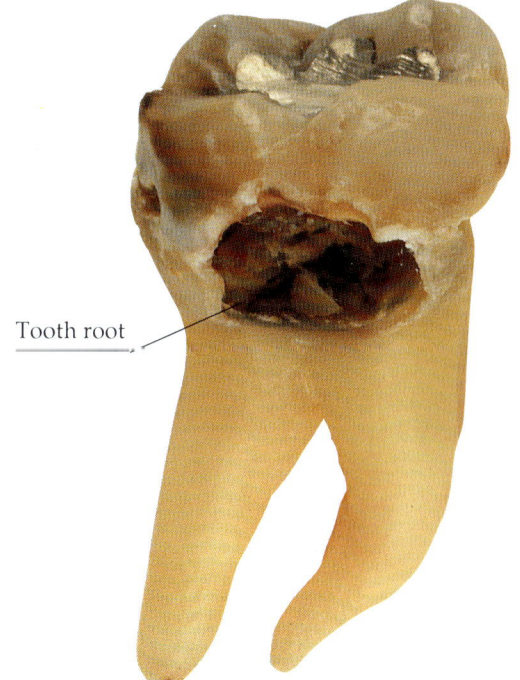

A teenager's decayed tooth that had to be extracted. The hole is too decayed to be filled

Tooth root

Open wide

Stand in front of a mirror and open your mouth.

How many teeth have you got? By using the picture opposite can you tell the names of each of your teeth?

By looking at the shape of your teeth, can you work out what happens to the food as it passes from your lips to your throat?

Bones

Our bones are always hidden from view. Because of this many people think that bones are simply hard, solid rods. But bones perform many important functions. They are constantly changing, renewing themselves and also creating new blood for our bodies.

Growing hands
As you grow, your hands become bigger as the bones get longer and thicker. Bones get longer by adding to the ends. The additions start off as extra layers of rubbery tissue called cartilage, and gradually this changes and hardens first into spongy bone, and later the outer regions harden into compact strong bone.

As you get older the cartilage on the end of each bone changes to spongy bone which then hardens to compact bone

You can see the marrow in this picture of an animal bone. The fresh blood cells give the marrow its red colour

Here the bone ends are cushioned by cartilage

This tissue contains the **blood vessels** that carry the blood to the bone

Fractures

The pictures below show how to think about a fractured bone in young people. Because the bone is still soft, it tends to splinter and split as shown by this new twig.

This kind of fracture can be bound together and it will heal quickly. Because of the likeness to plants, breaks in young bones are often called greenstick fractures.

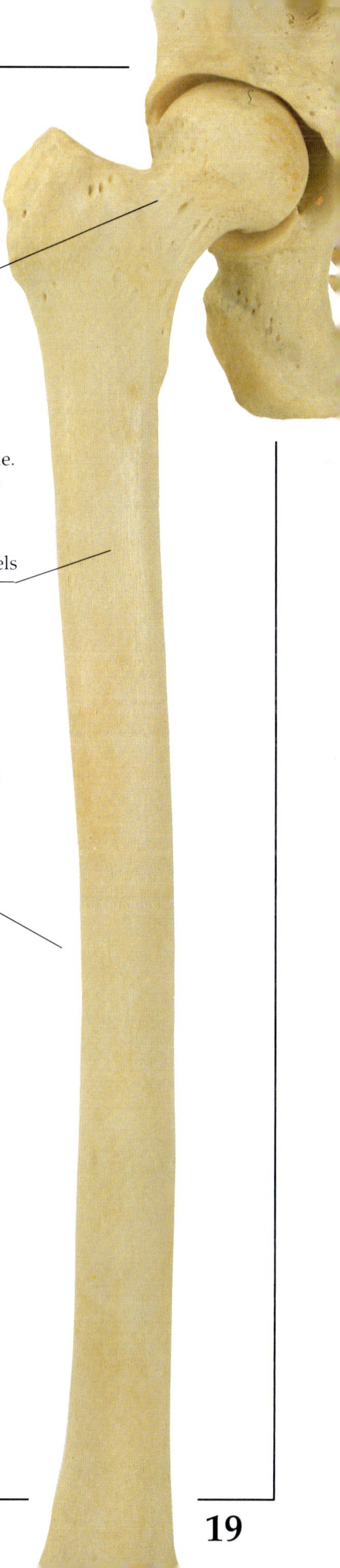

This is where breaks (fractures) are common in older people because this is where the greatest pressure is put on the bone and it is also quite thin

Femur, or thigh bone. Inside the hard case are the live marrow cells fed with blood through blood vessels

Some fractures occur here in young people where the bone is thin

Brittle bones

The bones of very young children are still relatively soft. This is the reason why younger people can take hard knocks without breaking their bones.

All bones change gradually through our lives. This is done by the cells inside the bone marrow.

When the bone is fully grown the material that makes the outside of the bone begins to harden and go more brittle. This is the reason older people have to be more careful to protect themselves against broken bones.

Familiar feet

Do you ever think of the tough job your feet have to do?

We often forget how much we rely on our feet. In fact, feet change shape just as much as others parts of the body, but if they are not looked after while they are growing, many problems can result when you are an adult.

What feet do

Feet contain many small bones, much like hands. But they also contain many very strong muscles and quite tough tissues, especially on the soles of the feet.

Unlike the hands, all the toes group together. This makes a sturdy yet flexible shape that allows us to walk and run.

The bones in the feet will get pushed out of place if they are squeezed into tight shoes. A badly shaped foot cannot grow to give the support the body needs.

Pressure points

The ball and heel of the foot and the big toe press onto the ground more heavily than other areas.

The arch between the ball and heel gives the foot its springiness. If this was flat on the floor it would be harder to walk and more difficult to run.

As feet grow the arch often becomes more pronounced because the body puts more and more strain on this natural spring.

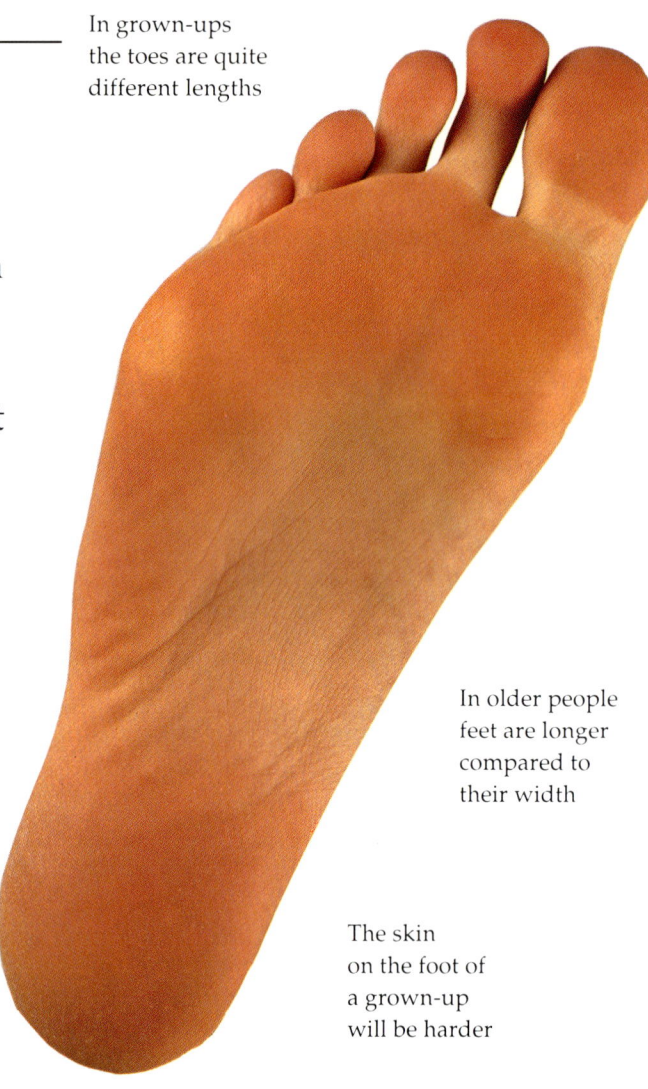

In grown-ups the toes are quite different lengths

In older people feet are longer compared to their width

The skin on the foot of a grown-up will be harder

Adult's foot

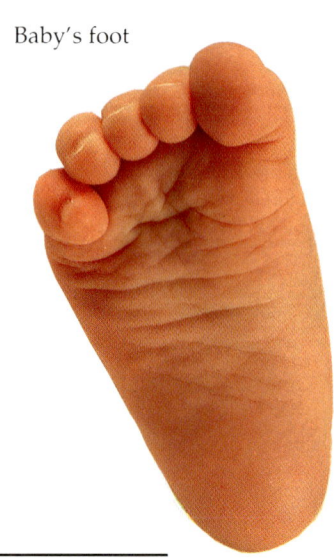

Baby's foot

Footprints

Look at your feet and think about their shape. It will be helpful if you press your bare foot into a tray of sand and make an imprint like the ones shown here. Then you can fill the impression with plaster of Paris or modelling plaster.

You can make a family of feet in this way. Get all the family to make an impression like the one shown here. It will make an interesting record to keep for the future.

Can you suggest why the shape and size of the feet change as people get older?

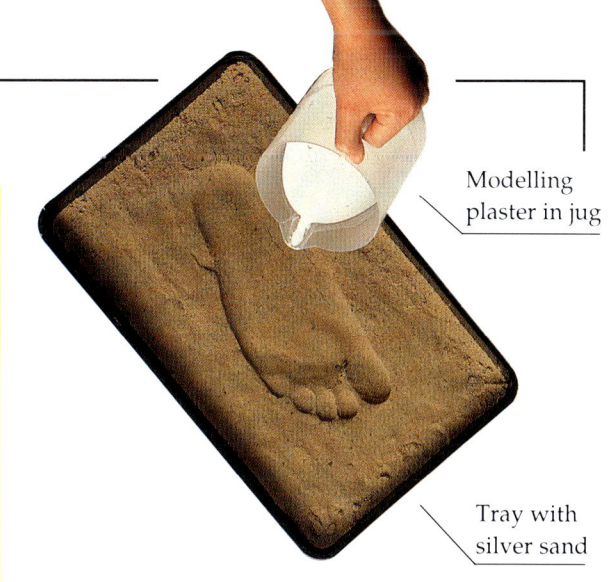

Modelling plaster in jug

Tray with silver sand

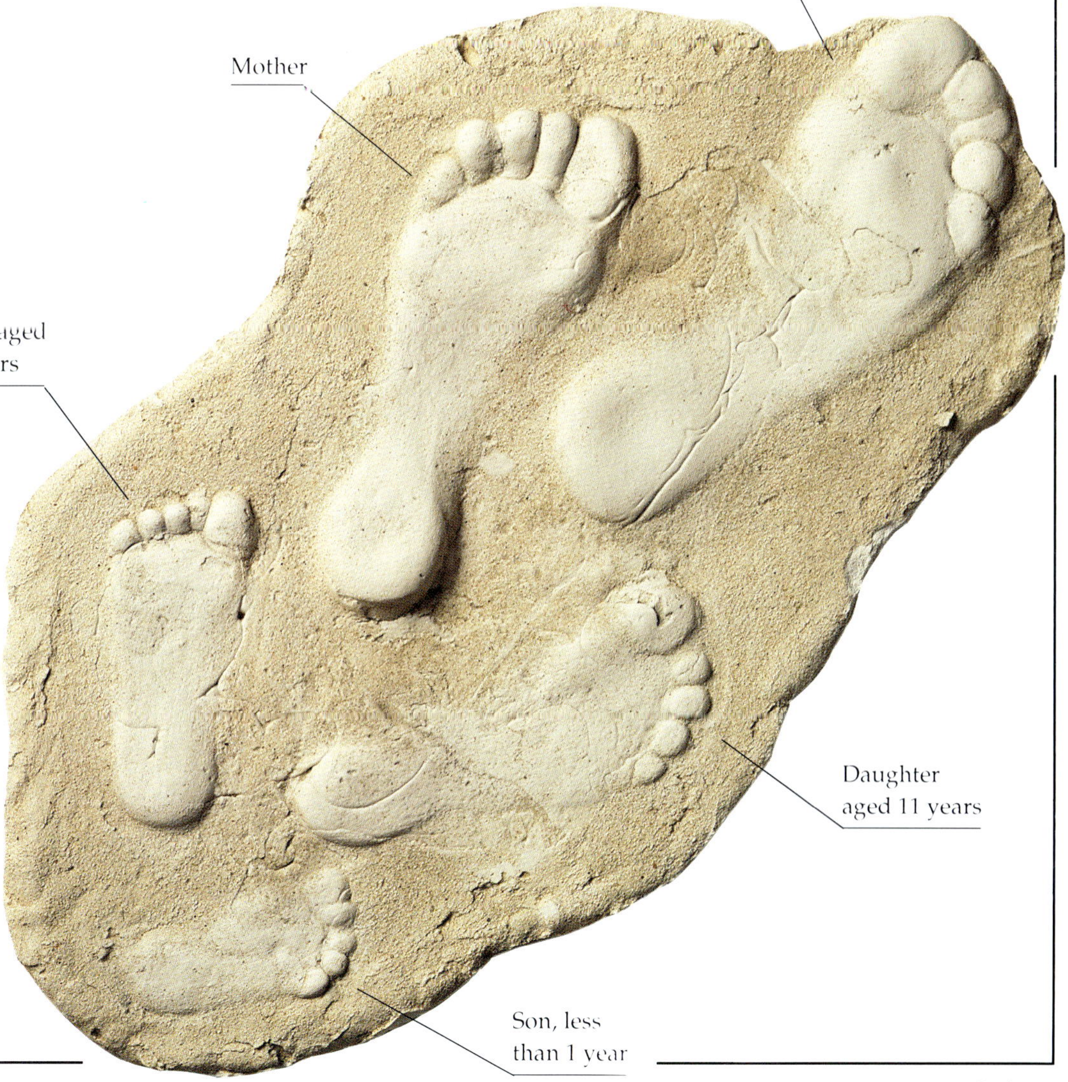

Mother

Father

Son, aged 5 years

Daughter aged 11 years

Son, less than 1 year

21

Filling out

As people get older, they finish growing taller and start to become more bulky. They are 'filling out'.

A thin person does not usually have the same strength in their muscles as a person who has more bulk.

As people get older they become more independent and do not need to rely on the help of their parents. They may start to have a family of their own. So adults need to be stronger so they can work to provide for and protect their own children.

Younger people do not look as different as adults

Women have slimmer waists because they store little fat there

Women have a finer skin than men because there are different chemicals at work just below the surface

Women store essential fat for energy around the hips and in the breasts. If they eat more food than they need, the extra fat is stored here

Filling different

Men change shape in different ways to women. A woman changes shape to prepare her body for pregnancy, childbirth, and for suckling her baby. One obvious change is the wider hips women have than men. You may have noticed that woman can often stand up for longer periods than men before they become tired. This is also a result of having stronger lower body muscles.

Men change shape and become broader in the shoulders. This gives them more strength for doing heavy jobs. This is the reason men can lift heavier weights than women.

Men develop more facial and body hair

Men develop bigger muscles

Men store essential fats around their waist. If they eat more food than they need, the extra fat is stored here

Hormones

As men and women develop, the many changes that take place in their bodies are controlled by special chemicals called **hormones**.

Men's hormones make them more hairy and give them bigger muscles. Women's hormones cause fat to be stored in various places, and give them smoother skin.

Growing older

Age 4

If you look through your family picture album you may see photographs of your parents and perhaps even your grandparents when they were much younger. They will have changed a lot from their early pictures. It's not just that their clothes are different, their faces, weight and their height will all have changed as well.

Everyone changes as they get older, although not as quickly as young people. Here are some of the changes.

First changes
The changes that have taken place to this girl between when she started school at age 4, and when she reached 11 are easy to spot. She has grown very much taller, for example. But can you see how the shape of her face has also changed? Her head is also smaller compared to her body because heads start large and grow only slowly.

Age 11

Age 34

The middle years

By the time people are in their teens they have almost reached their adult height. But their shape changes a lot. They begin to grow wider and it is easier to tell that men have a different shape to women.

As people reach their twenties they have become fully grown and changes take place much more slowly. It is difficult to tell exactly what changes have happened between age 34 and 54.

Age 54

The later years

The first signs of the later years may be greying hair, and skin which is not as smooth as in younger people. Older men also change in their hair pattern and some may start to shown signs of **balding**.

In later years people also become slightly smaller. This is because the tissue between the bones gets more compact. Bones also become more brittle.

People find they need more time to rest when they get older because their body systems do not make as much energy as when they were young. However, older people have gained a lot of knowledge and experience by having lived many years.

Your family changes

Look back through the pictures that your family have kept. Look at how each person has changed through the years. Do they show the same pattern of changes as those shown in the pictures here?

25

Hatching out

Some animals, such as birds, start life in an egg. Inside the shell are all the life-giving foods that the animal will need.

Inside the shell great changes occur as the animal's body develops. A chick even grows its feathers while inside the egg. Then, when the time is right, the animal hatches itself and emerges into the world.

The egg
The egg contains a yolk, which is the main source of food for the growing chick. The white provides only a small amount of food. Its main job is to provide a place for the chick to develop.

These swan's chicks are just emerging from their shells. The chick uses its beak to peck through and break the shell. Notice how the tightly packed bodies are limp when they emerge. The bones will soon become harder and stronger and the chick will find it easier to move about within a few hours

Down to feathers
A hatched chick looks very bedraggled because its feathers are still wet with the remains of the egg white. But this soon dries to give a coat of fine **down** which traps air and keeps the chick warm.

For many weeks the chick is unable to look after itself because it cannot see and the stumpy wings cannot be used to fly. Its parents have to make regular trips to find it suitable food.

Leaving the nest
The first steps to flying are difficult and many practice flappings of wings may be needed before the young birds are brave enough to try their first flight.

Baby blackbirds waiting for food

Young Sparrowhawks testing their wings

From water to land

Some creatures spend the first part of their life cycle in water and their adult life on land. Because water and land are so different, the same body shape cannot be used throughout life and major changes are needed.

Frogs and toads, for example, have to change dramatically from a fish-like creature with gills and a tail, to an air breathing creature with lungs and powerful legs.

These adult frogs are mating. The female will produce many hundreds of eggs which are **fertilized** in the water by the male. Each frog is about nine centimetres long

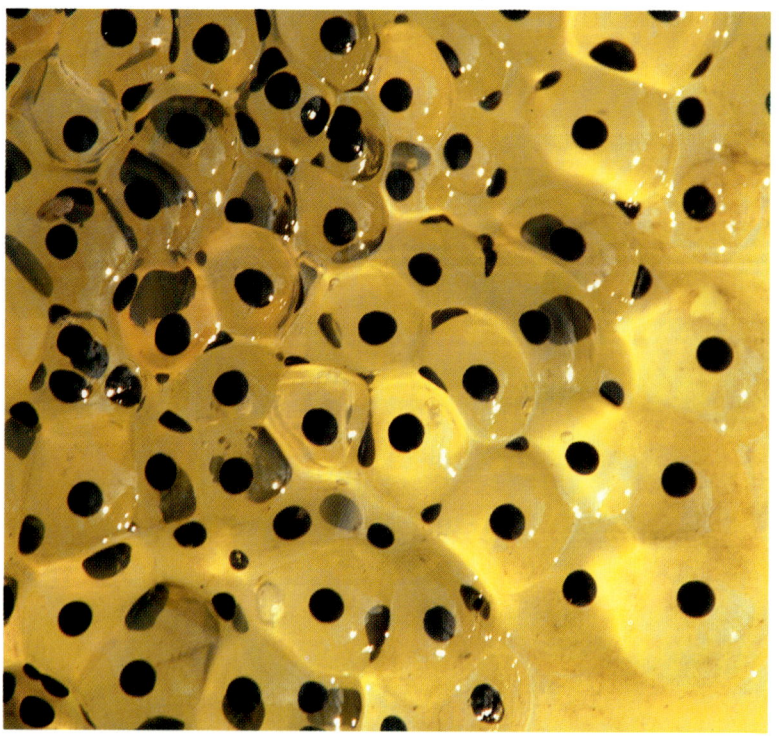

Frog spawn
The jelly-like eggs produced by frogs are stuck together. To keep them safe they are also stuck to reeds and other plants in the shallows of river banks and ponds.

The centre of each egg contains a black cell which gradually divides and changes shape until it becomes a tadpole.

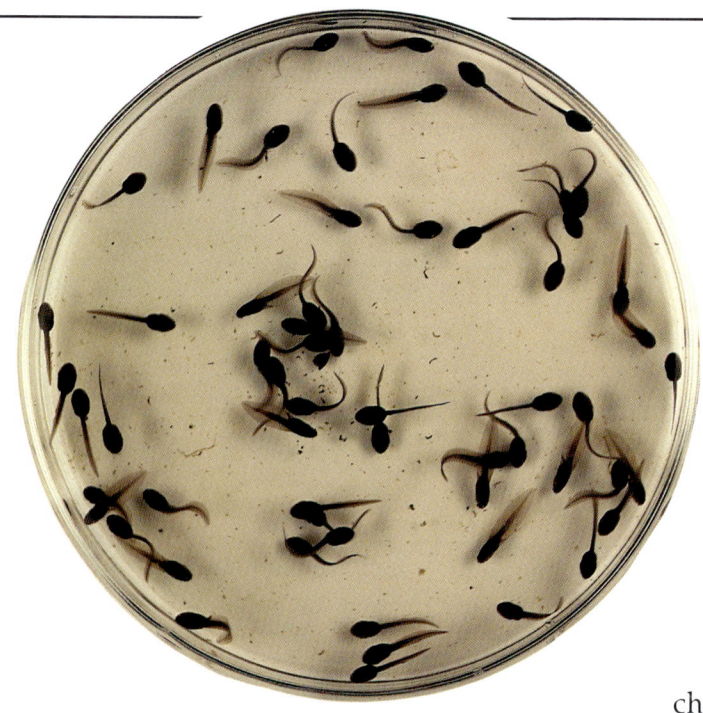

These are very young tadpoles, each less than a centimetre long

Tadpoles

Tadpoles are the first swimming stage of a frog. As soon as it hatches from the egg it develops a sucker-like mouth, a finned tail and gills to allow it to breath in water.

At first the tadpole lives by eating weeds, but later it changes and begins to eat insects.

About five weeks after hatching, the tadpoles start to grow rear legs and later, front legs. After this the jaw begins to change and the tadpole looks more and more like an adult frog.

Eventually it replaces its gills with lungs and the tail gradually shrinks. Now it can leave the water as a fully developed frog.

Tadpole watching

You can watch tadpoles in an aquarium. Make sure you do not keep too many tadpoles together or they will start to eat one-another. There should be a supply of weed to eat and eventually the adult frogs will need stones that stick up out of the water to sit on.

Tadpole changes take about three months. Make sure the water is kept clean all this time and return the frogs safely to the place where you found the tadpoles when you have finished watching them grow.

This tadpole is about four weeks old. It has reached about four centimetres in length

29

A brand new body

The change from a caterpillar to a butterfly or moth is one of the most spectacular in the natural world. The fat caterpillar, with its rows of feet and huge appetite, suddenly changes into a **chrysalis** or a **cocoon**.

When the butterfly or moth climbs out of the chrysalis or cocoon, it is a delicate winged insect with only six legs. Its future life may be so short, it may not be able to feed at all.

A caterpillar. The body grows so quickly it has to **moult** its skin several times before it is fully developed

Mouth

Legs with hooks on the feet to hold the caterpillar tight to the leaf

Special **camouflage** or defensive patterns

Metamorphosis

The change from egg through caterpillar and pupa to butterfly or moth is a very striking form of change, or **metamorphosis**.

The eggs are laid in clusters, often on the underside of a leaf. This leaf is chosen carefully to be the favourite food of the emerging caterpillar.

When the caterpillars (also called larvae) hatch from their eggs they immediately begin eating. Soon the tiny caterpillars are munching their way through the leaves, growing fatter and fatter by the day.

A butterfly emerging from its chrysalis

Chrysalis

Unseen change

When a caterpillar is fully developed it is ready to change into a pupa, or chrysalis. Some species attach themselves to stems with a silken thread and then wrap themselves in a silken case.

The case hardens and the pupa looks dead as it hangs on a branch. But inside the fat caterpillar completely rearranges its body and develops wings, sometimes within the space of just a few days.

Beautiful awakening

The butterfly or moth breaks its way out of the chrysalis or cocoon and then stands still on the stem while it pumps blood into its wings and lets them dry out. As soon as the wings are dry the insect, now transformed, begins its flight.

The job of the butterfly or moth is to seek a mate and lay eggs. The coloured wings will help it recognise a mate.

Some moths and butterflies can suck nectar as food and they may live for several months. Others have no mouths and live for just a few short days.

Two pairs of wings held upright at rest

A butterfly

Markings to attract a mate and sometimes to prevent attack

Antennae

Six legs

31

Making room for growth

People are examples of animals with backbones. We have our skeleton inside our bodies and we grow round it. Many other creatures have their bodies arranged with the skeleton on the outside, as for example a crab. This is often called a shell. A shell can be good for protection, but some shells cannot be made to grow. So many creatures have to shed their skeleton and grow a new one. Others shed skins or grow bigger shells.

Scale moult
Snakes have an internal skeleton, but they also have a protective skin made of hard scales. Because the scales do not grow a snake must shed its skin from time to time in a process called moulting.

First the skin round the lips is loosened, then it crawls out of its old skin, turning it inside out in the process.

A crab has a fixed shell which does not grow. From time to time it must shed the old shell, allowing the skin to harden into a new shell

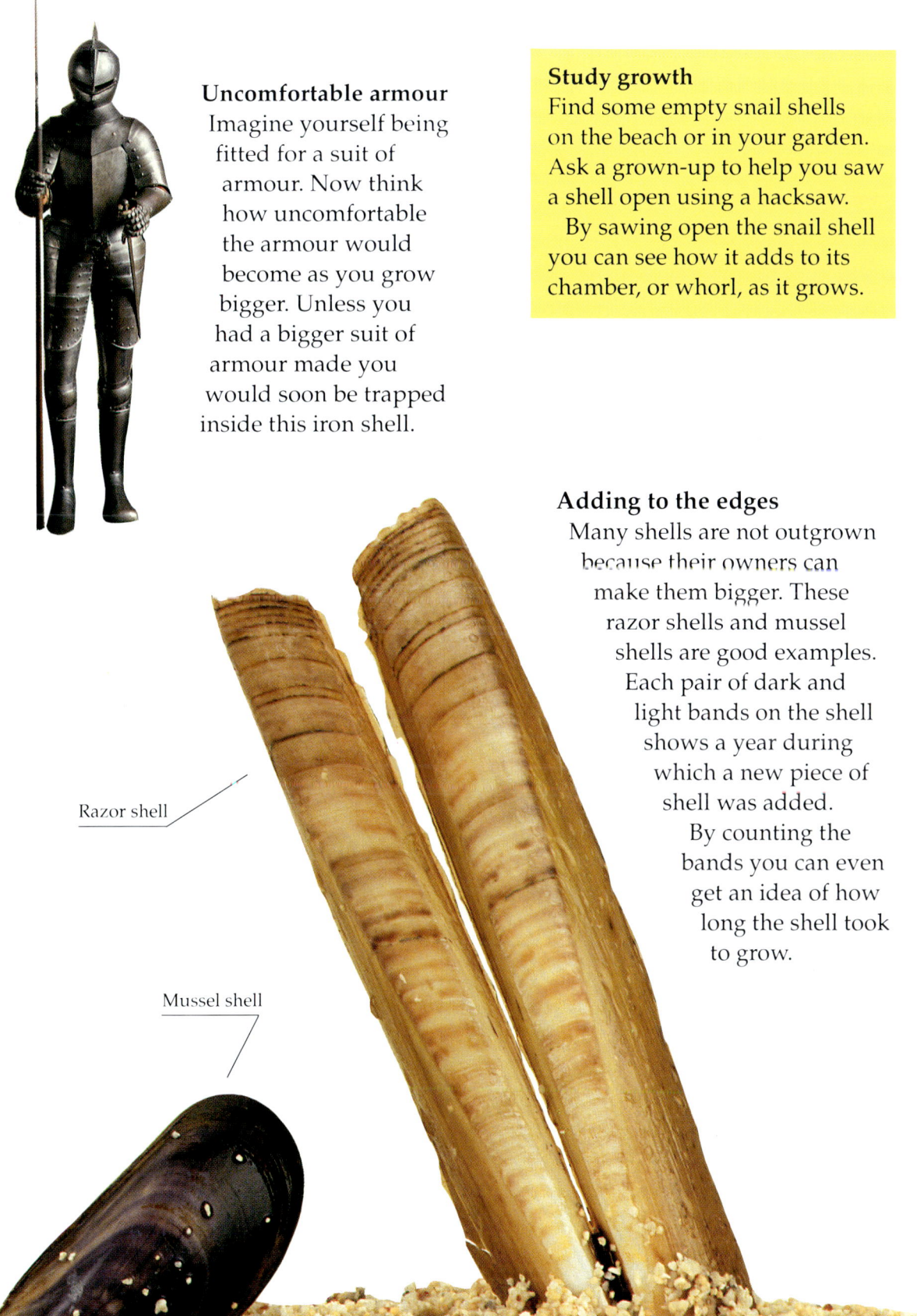

Uncomfortable armour
Imagine yourself being fitted for a suit of armour. Now think how uncomfortable the armour would become as you grow bigger. Unless you had a bigger suit of armour made you would soon be trapped inside this iron shell.

Study growth
Find some empty snail shells on the beach or in your garden. Ask a grown-up to help you saw a shell open using a hacksaw.

By sawing open the snail shell you can see how it adds to its chamber, or whorl, as it grows.

Adding to the edges
Many shells are not outgrown because their owners can make them bigger. These razor shells and mussel shells are good examples. Each pair of dark and light bands on the shell shows a year during which a new piece of shell was added.

By counting the bands you can even get an idea of how long the shell took to grow.

Razor shell

Mussel shell

Fishy changes

When fish hatch out of their eggs they are so tiny you can see right through them. At this time they have no colour to their skins, and no streamlined shape.

They quickly change in all kinds of ways, some developing spectacular colours, others fierce teeth and some, such as plaice, even turning their eyes completely round in their heads.

Eggs and larvae

Fish hatch from eggs, seen here clustered together. You can see the eyes of the unborn fish (called **embryo**) in the unhatched eggs.

Newly born fish (larvae) remain fixed to their yolk sacs which they use as food during the first days of life. However, they soon develop proper mouths and then they can feed on small insects.

Look closely at the picture of salmon eggs hatching and you will be able to see some of the internal organs of the larvae. The red lines are the main blood vessels.

You can also see the eyes, the start of the tail and the fins on the back (dorsal fins) and those on the underside (bottom fins).

When fish hatch out of their eggs they are tiny and you can often see right through them. At this time they have no colour to their skins

Young fish
Young fish are still very small. The one in this picture is about one centimetre long. Yet it has already developed scales, all its fins and some of its markings.

Fully-grown fish
The fully-grown fish has all its markings. They are designed for display and attracting a mate. Some also help with camouflage.

Adult fish are deeper and thicker than their young. This is because they have developed larger muscles to help them swim quickly through the water.

See scales grow
Scales are made of bone and designed to protect the body. The scales have no colour; the colour patterns are made in the skin below the scales.

Sharks scales do not grow and they have to be moulted so that larger ones can replace them. Most fish, however, have scales which grow with the fish. If you look at a scale of a dead fish through a hand lens or microscope, you can see the ridges that show where the scales have grown.

This fully-grown fish is about 6 centimetres long

The paired fins near the front of the fish are equivalent to the arms and legs of a land animal

Gills develop to help the fish filter oxygen from the water so that it can breath

35

Games they play

Pouncing: learning to spring to catch its prey. Notice the crouched shape of the body and how the claws are out

Capturing: learning to capture the prey by bringing it closer to the body. Now it is under control and can be killed

Eating: By chewing on the rope the jaw muscles become stronger. The kitten is now resting on its side after the effort of the capture

All **mammals** learn a lot by playing games. At the same time as a kitten is playing with a piece of string, or puppies romping together, they are learning as well as playing.

Playing helps them to get stronger muscles, to learn how to catch their food and to learn how to work together. Playing games also teaches them which one is boss, and helps them to find their place in the group.

Kittens and puppies
A kitten plays a different learning game to a puppy. This is because cats are lone hunters while dogs hunt in packs. Their games help them to learn how to catch their prey. Cats use their sharp claws to catch food, but dogs rely on their teeth.

Training your pet
Pets are better company when they have been trained. This means helping them to understand how to fit into our patterns of life.

Remember that a dog likes to be part of a pack; it will not like to be left alone. Cats are naturally 'loners' and they are certainly harder to train.

A dog learns best when your instructions are kept to simple words. It will easily learn that you are boss if you use a firm voice and say and do the same things all the time.

Above all be patient. Animals learn best from friendship rather than anger.

Who is boss?
As these kittens tumble about they are learning all the skills needed to catch and hold on to their prey.

Each kitten must also learn how to live with other cats and to find out how to defend its **territory**.

The rough and tumble playing that seems such fun is also a game of life.

Remember:
a pet is for life

Getting noticed

A special display
Male birds must attract females if they are to mate.
To do this they have to prove they are worthy partners.
Many birds develop special feathers which can be roughled. A peacock is a fine example.
Others have pouches that can be made larger when a female comes near – a real case of showing off.

As animals become older, most of them go in search of a mate. But attracting a mate is not easy. Many animals find the best way is to develop bright colours and advertise!

A frigate bird making its pouch as large as it can

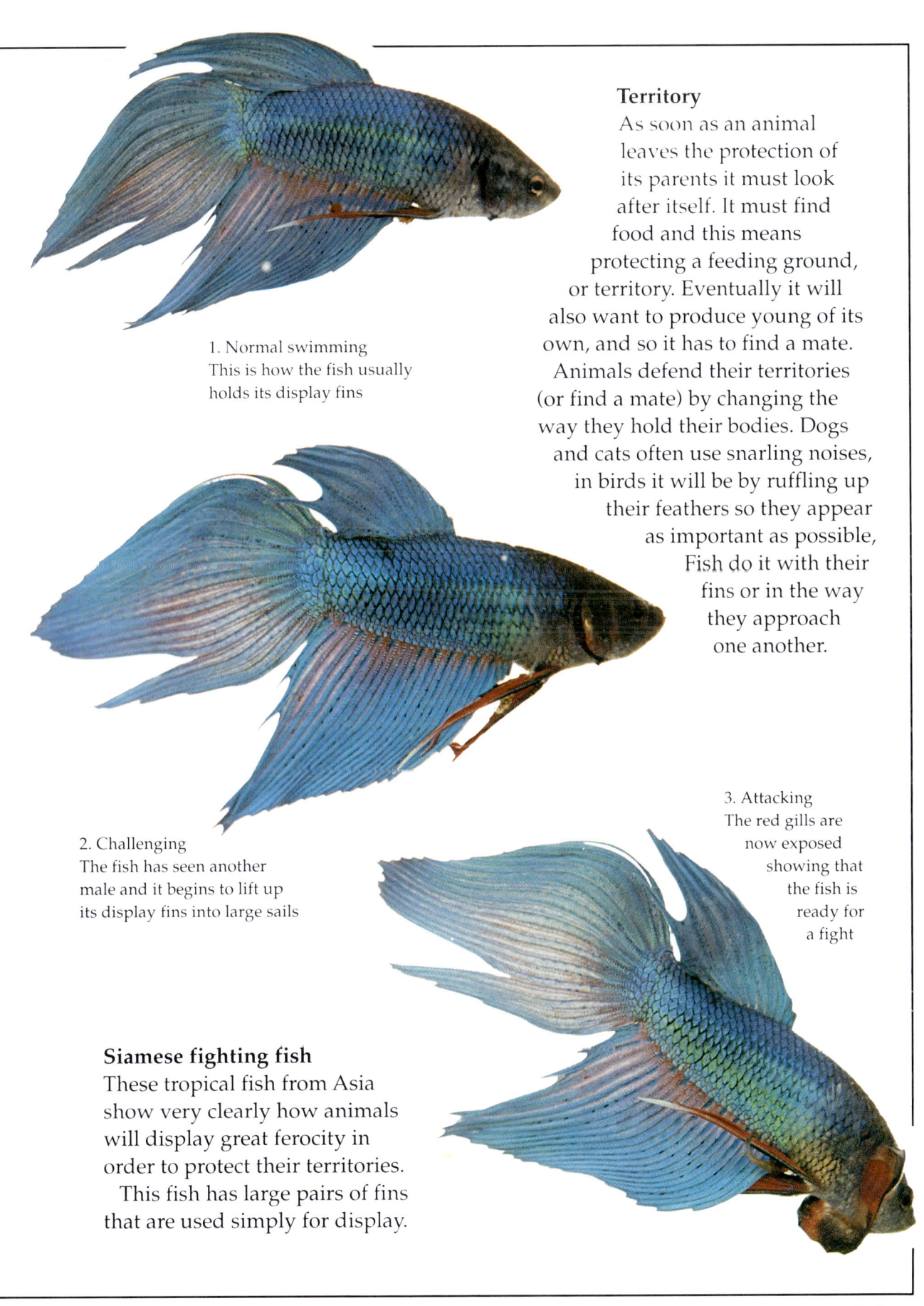

1. Normal swimming
This is how the fish usually holds its display fins

Territory
As soon as an animal leaves the protection of its parents it must look after itself. It must find food and this means protecting a feeding ground, or territory. Eventually it will also want to produce young of its own, and so it has to find a mate. Animals defend their territories (or find a mate) by changing the way they hold their bodies. Dogs and cats often use snarling noises, in birds it will be by ruffling up their feathers so they appear as important as possible, Fish do it with their fins or in the way they approach one another.

2. Challenging
The fish has seen another male and it begins to lift up its display fins into large sails

3. Attacking
The red gills are now exposed showing that the fish is ready for a fight

Siamese fighting fish
These tropical fish from Asia show very clearly how animals will display great ferocity in order to protect their territories.
This fish has large pairs of fins that are used simply for display.

39

Sprouting into life

As seeds develop into plants they show many of the changes that happen during growing. Each seed starts by relying on its built-in energy.

As the seed swells, chemical changes produce the first signs of life. A plant must seek a source of food and water, then it must search for light before its own 'internal battery' is used up.

The leaf opens out just like an umbrella. The veins in the leaves becoming stiff and holding the leaf out to the light

The leaf uses the energy from the Sun's rays to turn **nutrients** and water into the cells which make roots, stems and more leaves

Sprouting chestnut tree

The root is sent down to find water and nutrients before the stem shoots upwards. Notice how the stem already has a leaf as soon as it unfurls

The supply of nourishment from the seed is gone. Now the sapling must fend for itself

A seed that appears dry and lifeless starts to swell as soon as spring comes and the soil warms

The root develops many rootlets. Each one can search a separate piece of soil for water and nutrients

This beanarium has one species of bean growing on one side. There is a different species on the other side. Because they were put in the jar at the same time they make a fair test between which bean grows fastest

Part 1: Make a 'beanarium'
Beans grow quickly in a jar filled with water and you can see changes every day. To see how a bean grows, put some cotton wool in a jar. Make sure there is enough to hold a bean against the side of the jar as shown in this picture.

Put in a bean. A pair of tweezers will help you to place it nicely. Put it up the same way as the picture.

Now add water until there is about two centimetres in the bottom of the jar. The cotton wool will soak up moisture and make the bean wet.

If you put different types of beans around the sides of the jar you can see which beans emerge first.

A bean with its first leaf

Part 2: Record the changes
Make sketches, or take pictures of the beans as they grow. Find out if they have the same growth stages as the chestnut on the opposite page.

Beans need nourishment to grow and they must be planted in soil. When the bean roots reach the bottom of the jar you can plant the beans in a pot and watch the way they grow larger.

41

Leaves

Plants need to have lots of ways of protecting themselves at every stage of life. Once a plant has begun to grow and send down roots it is fixed there until it dies. So it must make sure it has many ways of surviving.

Plants use leaves to make the energy they need to survive. But in cool climates or very dry climates leaves can present the plant with a problem. Leaves can be killed by frost or they can wilt in a drought.

Many plants have leaves that grow when the warm or wet weather arrives. When the cold or drought arrives, the leaves are then shed. These are **deciduous** plants.

Bursting buds
The hard wood of a twig looks quite dead. It seems impossible that new life could burst through. The hard scales that cover the buds are there to protect these new growths, so they have to be thick and tough.

The first sign of a new season's growth is when the scales split apart and the new bud can be seen.

The first leaf

Flower

Swelling bud still covered with scales

Tough survivors
The emerging leaves are soft and many are covered in a delicate fur. They have to grow tough surfaces that can stand up to being blown by the wind, pounded by the rain, or to prevent attack from insects or other animals wanting to eat them.

As they toughen up the leaves become noticeably darker.

Leaves are tightly packed inside the buds. It takes time for them to open out

Emerging leaves
Leaves need to hold themselves up to capture the light. Leaves have stiff veins to help keep their shape. The leaf unfurls as it grows and as the veins stiffen.

The last stage
When the growing season comes to an end the leaves have finished their job. Now the tree begins to cut off the supply of water to the leaves and they go brown and begin to shrivel.

As the leaves finally fall the scar where they grew is closed over by new scales and next season's bud begins to grow.

43

Flowering and fruiting

A plant changes very rapidly when it is time to flower. At the right time of year, or when the right temperature is reached, a mechanism is triggered within the plant and buds are formed. The buds contain all the parts that will be needed to form flowers and seeds.

Attractive flower
As the flower opens fully the bright colours are able to attract insects. They are attracted by the colour, the scent and the nectar held inside the flower.

As the insect collects the nectar it leaves behind pollen collected from another plant. This fertilizes the flower.

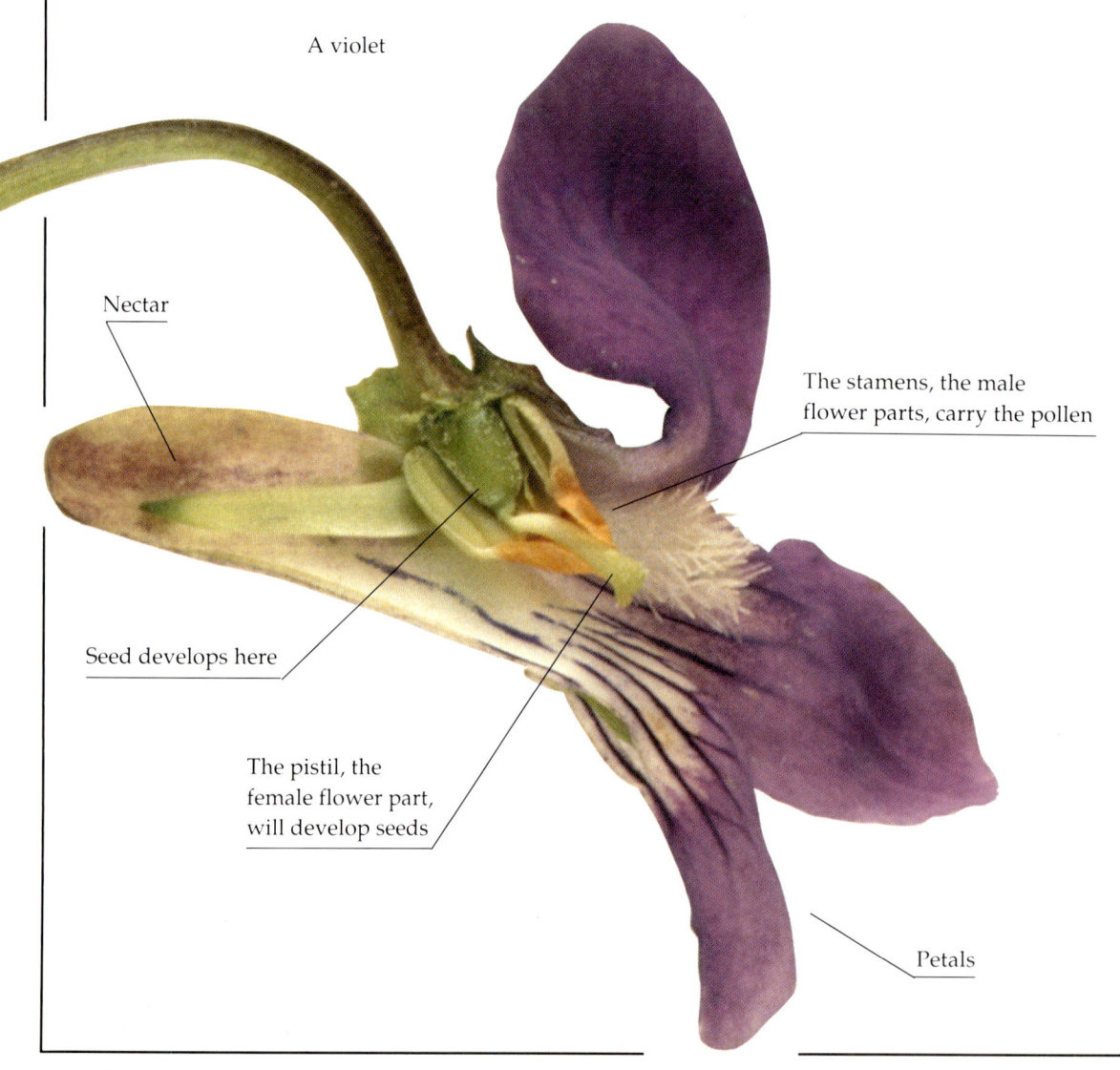

A violet

Nectar

The stamens, the male flower parts, carry the pollen

Seed develops here

The pistil, the female flower part, will develop seeds

Petals

44

Seeds develop   Seeds are carried away by the wind

As soon as the flower has been fertilized another trigger is set off inside the plant. The job of the flowers is over, and eventually they will wither and fall away. At the base of the flowers a seed pod begins to swell. Inside it lie the seeds that will provide the plants of the future

Keep a record of the change
It is easy to save flowers by pressing them. Start with a large sheet of white blotting paper. Put the flowers carefully on one side, making sure the petals are nicely laid out. Don't forget to press the wilting flowers as well, even though they may not be as pretty.

Write the date of collection on a label and keep it alongside.

Fold the other half of the blotting paper and put the package carefully under some heavy books for a few weeks. The blotting paper will soak up the moisture and allow the flowers to be preserved.

The dried flowers can be mounted onto white card with glue. Compare any changes that have occurred between opening and wilting.

The bud covers are called sepals. As they open the petals burst out

As soon as fertilization takes place the flower petals fall away

Dandelion

Opening buds

New words

average
the word used to describe a value that is thought to be normal. The average is calculated, for example, by adding all the heights of a group together and then dividing by the number in the group

bacteria
this is a name given to a large group of microscopic organisms. Some use sugars on the teeth as food and release acids that rot tooth enamel

balding
the gradual loss of hair from the head because the hair producing cells in the scalp begin to die. It is a common feature of men, but very rare in women

blood vessels
the tubes that carry blood from the heart to the rest of the body and back again. Blood is red when it has plenty of oxygen

camouflage
a pattern of shapes and colours that makes it difficult to spot an animal in its natural surroundings

cells
the basic building blocks of animals and plants. Cells contain all the information necessary for life.
Our bodies are constantly making new cells to replace the dead ones

chrysalis
the silken case made by a caterpillar as it prepares to turn into a butterfly

cocoon
the silken wrapping or case made by a caterpillar as it prepares to turn into a moth.

co-ordination
the process of doing many linked things at the same time. For example, when we walk we normally co-ordinate the movement of our arms and legs to keep our bodies balanced

deciduous
when plants shed their leaves for part of the year and stop growing they are said to be deciduous. Many trees are deciduous to allow them to survive a harsh winter or a drought

down
the very soft underfeathers of a bird. Chicks start life covered with down, but as they grow older the larger body and flight feathers grow through the down and hide it

embryo
the word used to describe any animal or plant in the first stages of life, before it develops its final form

fertilize
the process of bringing female and male parts together in order to produce new life

gills
these are the special structures that allow fish and some other animals to absorb oxygen out of the water. Gills do the same job as lungs in land animals

hormone
A hormone is a chemical messenger which is made in a special gland. There are glands scattered all over the body. However, some glands in women and men are different and this is what causes them to develop differently as they become grown-ups

incisor
these are the sharp, chisel-shaped teeth at the front of the mouth. Their job is to cut into the food so that pieces can be torn off

mammal
an animal with hair that gives birth to live young (as opposed to, for example, laying eggs)

metamorphosis
a complete change that happens to an animal as it grows up to be an adult. The word metamorphosis is used only for dramatic changes such as caterpillar to insect or tadpole to frog

molar
the back teeth which are broad and designed to crush food. The ridges of the upper molars fit closely into the valleys of the lower molars. You can feel this close fit when you rub your teeth together

moult
a period when animals loose all, or a large part, of their coats or skin. Dogs moult by shedding many hairs, snakes moult by shedding their entire skin

nerve
cells that carry electrical messages to the brain. Nerves are extremely sensitive and if touched directly can cause considerable pain

nutrients
the special substances that are needed to help build new cells. Plants get their nutrients directly from the soil; animals get nutrients by eating plants or other animals

placenta
a piece of special tissue that is attached to the inside of the womb. The baby is attached to the placenta by the umbilical cord

territory
the area that an animal tries to keep for its own use. Males will fight over territories because once they have mated, the territory must have enough food to support male, females and offspring

womb
the place inside the female's belly where the baby develops. The womb, or uterus, is a tube-like muscle which is strong enough to push the baby out when it is time to give birth

47

Index

average 12, 13, 14, 15, 46

baby 6, 7, 8, 20
bacteria 17, 46
balding 25, 46
blood vessels 18, 19, 46
bone 15, 18-19, 25
bud 42, 43, 45
butterfly 31

camouflage 30, 35, 46
cartilage 18
caterpillar 30
cells 6, 46
chrysalis 30, 31, 46
claws 36
cocoon 30, 31, 46
co-ordination 9, 46
crawling 9

deciduous 42, 46
display 38-9
dorsal fin 34
down 27, 46

egg 26, 28, 30, 31, 34
embryo 34, 46
energy 25, 40

fat 22, 23
feathers 26-7
feet 14, 20-1
femur 19
fertilize 28, 44, 46
fin 34, 5
fish 34, 35, 39
flower 44
frog 28

gills 28, 29, 35, 47
grandparents 24

hair 14, 15, 25
hands 18
hatch 26, 30
height 12, 13, 15
hips 22, 23
hormones 23, 46

incisors 16, 17, 46
kitten 36-7

larvae 30, 34
leaves 40, 42, 43
lungs 29

mammals 36, 47
marrow 18, 19
mate 28, 38, 39
metamorphosis 30, 47
milk teeth 16
molar 16, 47
moult 30, 32, 47
muscles 14, 22

nails 15
nectar 31, 44
nerve 17, 47
nutrients 40, 47

parents 24
placenta 7, 47
pollen 44
pregnant 6
profile 11

proportion 10
pupa 31
puppy 36

root 40

sapling 40
scale 35, 43
seed 40, 44, 45
sense 8, 9
shark 35
shell 26, 32, 33
silk 31
skeleton 32
skill 8-9
snail 33
snake 32
survival 10, 42, 43

tadpole 28-9
teeth 16-17
territory 37, 39, 47
touch 8

umbilical cord 7

veins 40, 43

weight 14, 15
wings 27, 31
womb 6, 47

yolk 26, 34

48